Original title:
Citrus Chronicles

Copyright © 2025 Creative Arts Management OÜ
All rights reserved.

Author: Sophia Kingsley
ISBN HARDBACK: 978-1-80586-327-4
ISBN PAPERBACK: 978-1-80586-799-9

Twilight Citrus

Under the glow of a setting sun,
Lemons giggle, oh what fun!
Oranges dance, they spin and sway,
While grapefruits plot to steal the day.

Squirrels in hats, they join the spree,
Juggling fruits, oh can't you see?
Citrus laughter fills the air,
Fruitful jokes without a care.

In the Heart of Oranges

In a grove where oranges play,
A lemon laughed and rolled away.
Tangerines, so plump and bright,
    Held a party every night.

Grapefruits told the funniest tales,
While lemons sailed in tiny gales.
Peeling laughter, zest set free,
   In this land, such glee to see!

Rind and Reflection

A lime looked in the mirror sleek,
"Am I sweet or am I cheek?"
Oranges chimed, "You're quite the zest!"
"Let's have a competition, who's the best?"

With rinds that gleamed in the sun's embrace,
Each fruit puffed up, puffing their case.
But a banana slipped and stole the show,
Leaving the citrus in laughter's glow.

A Symphony of Zest

A violin made from tangerine,
Played tunes that were quite obscene.
Lemons tapped on spoons so loud,
As grapefruits formed a dancing crowd.

The zestful notes filled the air,
Melodies made with fruity flair.
A symphony of laughter rang,
As all the citrus fruits went tang!

Bitter-Sweet Reflections

In the garden of zest, where the sun shines bright,
Lemons tell tales of their sour delight.
Oranges chuckle, their peels all aglow,
While grapefruits gossip, putting on a show.

A citrus parade where the laughter's so sweet,
They dance on the branches with little foot feet.
Limes roll their eyes, making faces so bold,
As the lemons share secrets that never get old.

Lemonade Dreams

Sipping on sunshine in a glass so cold,
Sugar and water turn bitter to gold.
Each drop of laughter, a slice on the rim,
With every sweet giggle, our spirits won't dim.

Mixing in stories of summers gone by,
Citrus concoctions that whisper and sigh.
A splash of mischief, a twist of a cheek,
In lemonade dreams, we all find our peak.

The Citrus Orchard's Tale

In an orchard so noisy, the fruit came alive,
Chatter and chuckles, they're thriving, they strive.
The oranges blurt out the juiciest news,
While the lemons throw shade, just to bemuse.

Under branches alive with a citrusy spree,
They joke about weather, as sweet as can be.
The bees join the fun, buzzing in delight,
In this orchard of laughter, everything's bright.

Ripe Revelations

A fruit bowl of wisdom, all ripe for the day,
One lemon grumbles, "Why do we decay?"
With a wink from a peach, the answer came clear,
"It's all in the zest, my dear, have no fear!"

So gather your limes with their limey keen eye,
For life's too short to just sit and comply.
Each slice of our stories is juicy and grand,
In this world of citrus, together we stand.

In the Orchard's Embrace

In an orchard full of zest,
Lemons dance with such a jest,
Oranges giggle, apples grin,
Kicking off a fruity spin.

Cherries chat with whispered glee,
While grapefruits try to climb a tree,
Limes roll down with quite a flare,
Creating laughter everywhere.

The Sweetest Seasons

Summer brings the juicy cheer,
With every slice, laughter near,
Lemonade stands lined in rows,
Where sticky fingers steal the shows.

Autumn sends the tangy treats,
Pumpkins join, with citrus beats,
With pies adorned in zestful hype,
The flavor's just a perfect type.

Mimosas and Memories

Mimosas bubbling, parties bright,
Citrus colors, such a sight,
Friends toast with a fruity laugh,
Sharing jokes while sipping half.

Brunch becomes a zesty dance,
With every sip, a merry chance,
To mix and mingle, sip and swirl,
Bright orange juice, oh what a whirl!

The Dance of the Zest

Lemons twirl, oranges prance,
In a zesty, fun-filled dance,
Grapefruits hop, limes do the twist,
Who knew fruit could be like this?

Bouncing high, they play around,
In the sunlight, joy is found,
Their laughter fills the sunny skies,
In this vibrant, fruity surprise.

Serendipity in Slices

Zesty peels fall like confetti,
Lemon laughs, oh-so petty.
Oranges roll in playful heaps,
Tangerines make silly leaps.

Mimosas spill on linen cloth,
Grapefruit giggles, no one scoffs.
A juicing party, fruit brigade,
Limes in hats, they've got it made!

Slicing smiles with every twist,
Citrus joys we can't resist.
Lemonade spills a sunny cheer,
Citrus slices, oh so dear!

In the bowl, a jaundiced dream,
Fruit parade, a vibrant theme.
Pineapples juggle, setting up,
For a punchline in a cup!

From Blossom to Beverage

From flower buds to fizzy swirls,
Bees draw nectar, dance, and twirl.
Lemon blossoms grinning bright,
Mocking petals, morning light.

A juicer's dream, oh what a scene,
Citrus streams, a vibrant green.
Limes in smoothies, bright and bold,
Stories of sweetness, long retold.

Oranges tumble in a chase,
Juice drips down, a lovely mess.
Rinds as hats for silly minds,
Fruitful fun, the best of kinds.

In a glass, a twist of fate,
Citrus soda on my plate.
Pineapple floats with cheeky flair,
A bubbly drink beyond compare!

Nectar of the Grove

Sunshine bottled, zest in hand,
Grove's laughter, oh so grand.
Lemonade rivers, waves of joy,
Sipping sunshine, not a ploy.

Grapefruits giggle, rolling round,
Juicy jewels fall to the ground.
Dancing limes with merry pride,
In this grove, there's no need to hide.

With every squeeze, a pop of fun,
Citrus games, we've just begun.
Pulp and laughter mix and swirl,
Fruits in motion, watch them twirl!

From grove to glass, the tale unfolds,
Sippy cups and citrus holds.
A nectar cheer from tree to tongue,
In this garden, we are young!

The Fruitful Journey

Tripping on peels, what a sight,
Fruits on a journey, pure delight.
Bananas lead with carefree grace,
Mangoes wink, a fruity race.

Grapes in line, they start to dance,
Fruit salad comes, take a chance.
Tasting troubles, less serious,
Sippin' smiles, so mysterious.

Lemons plot and scheme away,
Dreaming of a zesty day.
Citrus tales spun in the breeze,
Tales of laughter, sure to please.

From tree to table, on we roam,
This fruity journey, feel at home.
Joy in every bite we take,
Citrus giggles, never fake!

The Squeeze of Summer

In the sun, a lemon grins,
It laughs at all the juice within.
A pitcher waits, a glass in hand,
Droplets dance like grains of sand.

Oranges roll, a laughter spree,
They race around, so wild and free.
Lemonade spills a sunny cheer,
While ice cubes giggle, oh so near.

Grapefruits wear their little hats,
They sip from straws like little cats.
A twist of rind, a twist of fate,
A pithy joke, we celebrate.

Lime joins in with playful rhyme,
Chiming in with zesty chime.
In this grand, fruity parade,
We'll cheer for every punchy trade.

Citrus in the Breeze

A mandarin sailed on a breeze,
Waving 'hello' like autumn leaves.
Delightful scents drift in the air,
A fragrant carnival; do you dare?

Lemons laugh, they roll and bounce,
In a bowl where oranges flounce.
The wind tells tales of what could be,
As zest-filled dreams embrace the spree.

Lime weighs in with cheeky charms,
It tickles taste buds, rings the alarms.
As laughter echoes through the grove,
The humor in the zest we love.

Grapefruits gather, telling jokes,
About the time they turned to smokes.
In this garden of fruity schemes,
We find the joy in our zesty dreams.

Blossoms and Bitters

In a tree of blossoms bright,
Limes and oranges take to flight.
They play peek-a-boo with the sun,
In this orchard, joy weighs a ton.

Sweet aroma fills the air,
While grapefruits flirt without a care.
Bitter jokes are tossed around,
As fruits unite upon the ground.

Lemon zest, a playful sprite,
Turns a frown to sheer delight.
Mixing flavors, blending fun,
A punchline thrown, a race now run.

The blossoms giggle, petals swirl,
As citrus pals give life a twirl.
In every sip, in every bite,
We find the fun that feels just right.

Essence of Zest

A zesty wave from peel to core,
Brings laughter loud and spirits soar.
With every squeeze, a giggle blends,
As juice bursts forth, time transcends.

Limes prance on the kitchen floor,
While oranges strategize for war.
"Let's make a punch!" they all agree,
Squeezing joy so merrily.

Peels fly high like kites in spring,
With humorous tales they always bring.
A dash of whimsy, a splash of cheer,
We celebrate all year, my dear.

In this dance of sour and sweet,
Life's little joys can't be beat.
So come and share a laugh or two,
With fruit so bright, there's fun for you.

Slices of Sunlight

In the grove where lemons play,
They dance and twirl in sunny sway.
A lime once tried to join the fun,
But rolled away, forgot to run.

Orange laughs with zestful cheer,
While grapefruit grins from ear to ear.
The tangy beats, they skip and hop,
While citrus pals just can't quite stop.

A tangerine slipped on a peel,
Declared, "This fruit life is a steal!"
With citrus friends, the days are bright,
They share a giggle, pure delight.

So grab a spritz, let's toast with glee,
For in this grove, we're wild and free.
Our juicy tales, they flow like juice,
In laughter's bliss, we all let loose.

Juicy Whispers

In a bowl of fruits, they scheme and plot,
Whispering secrets in the sunny spot.
A sly kiwi, oh what a rascal,
Trying to sneak without a hassle.

Lemons giggle with tart delight,
While oranges quip, "We're out of sight!"
A pineapple wearing shades so cool,
Says, "Sunshine's here, let's all be a fool!"

The grapefruit jokes, "I'm quite a squeeze!"
As laughter floats upon the breeze.
Each fruit plays tricks until they fall,
In juicy whispers, we share it all.

So raise your peel to friendship's cheer,
In fruit-filled fun, we shed a tear.
Juicy tales, with laughter and zest,
In this orchard, we are truly blessed.

Orchard Dreams

Underneath the apple trees,
Lemons dream of ocean breeze.
"What if we could surf a wave?"
The oranges laugh, "Be brave, be brave!"

With a skateboard made of rind,
A crazy lemon's hard to find.
Tree branches sway in silly glee,
As cherries plan a jubilee.

A pear once tried to take a flight,
But landed funny, what a sight!
While berries sing a silly tune,
The orchard feels like a cartoon.

So let us frolic, let us dream,
In this garden, life's a gleam.
With hues of joy and laughter's reign,
These orchard dreams keep calling again.

Limoncello Lullabies

As night descends, the fruits unite,
They share their tales in soft twilight.
A nightly blend of zest and cheer,
With limoncello hugs, we're here!

The grapefruit hums a sleepy song,
While fruit flies dance along where they belong.
Pineapple snores, a tropical tune,
Underneath the watchful moon.

Lemons giggle in dream's embrace,
Imagining a wild fruit race.
"I'll be the champion!" they proclaim,
In sleepy smiles, they stake their claim.

So when stars twinkle in the sky,
And citrus dreams begin to fly,
We'll sip our drinks of lemon cheer,
And laugh together, year after year.

The Essence of Citrus

Lemons dancing on the shelf,
Who knew they had such stealth?
Oranges juggling by the window,
Just trying to steal the show!

Lime with a hat, feeling bold,
Squeezing jokes, or so I'm told.
Tangerines rolling on the floor,
Laughing at the fruits of yore.

Mandarin Murmurs

Mandarins whisper in the breeze,
Sharing secrets with such ease.
Their peels slip off like a prank,
Leaving juice—ah, the sweet flank!

With every squeeze, there's a giggle,
Fruit salad's now got a wiggle.
Citrus jokes, they always land,
In the orchard, it's quite grand.

Nectar of Nostalgia

Sipping juice from childhood days,
Reminiscing in silly ways.
Grandma's punch with extra zest,
A feast that just feels the best!

Sticky fingers and bright smiles,
Citrus flavors dance for miles.
Limes and lemons, how they tease,
Paint my memories with ease.

Grapefruit Gaze

Peering at my grapefruit friend,
Wondering where this will end.
Half a spoon, a sprinkle of sugar,
Yet still, I think it might be a booger!

Sour faces, a comical sight,
Pondering life in the morning light.
With every bite, a squirt of cheer,
Who knew breakfast could be so queer?

The Orchard's Heartbeat

In the orchard, fruit does sway,
A lemon said, "Let's have a play!"
The oranges giggled, oh what a sight,
While grapefruits danced into the night.

The limes rolled down a grassy hill,
Yelling, "Catch us! We've got the thrill!"
A tangerine juggled, a tricky feat,
While neighbors wondered, "Who can compete?"

A fruit fly joined, wearing a hat,
Said, "I'm the judge, just look at that!"
The laughter echoed as they performed,
In this zesty world, friendships were warmed.

With every giggle, their colors shone,
In the orchard's heart, they felt at home.
The fruits rejoiced, all worries ceased,
In this merry grove, they found their feast.

Zing of the Tropics

Oh what a zing in the tropical air,
Bananas wearing hats, without a care!
Papayas strummed on coconut strings,
While mangos danced, oh how they swing!

A parrot squawked, "Let's have a race!"
But the guavas just wanted to chill and brace.
With vibrant colors, laughter ran deep,
As the fruits came together, oh what a heap!

A lime spilled juice with a cheeky grin,
As pineapples joked, "Let's do it again!"
Oranges rolled, making quite a scene,
Here in the tropics, no one's mean!

Under the sun, the fun won't cease,
With a splash, a zestful peace.
And when the day turns into night,
The fruits will laugh, each with delight.

Breathe in the Zest

Breathe in the zest, what a treat,
Lemons start singing to the beat.
A little lime, sporting a grin,
Said, "Let's see where this fun begins!"

They all cramped up in a shopping cart,
With jingles and laughter, a fruity art.
The cherries rocked, the berries twirled,
On this funny adventure, oh what a world!

An orange slipped, fell on its peel,
Said, "Oops! Didja see that real wheel?"
The lemons roared in their sunny delight,
Saying, "Join our laughter, it's quite a sight!"

They giggled and jostled, made quite a mess,
Spilling seeds, oh what a stress!
But every slip brought cheerful cheers,
In this zestful jam, they had no fears.

The Citrus Canvas

On the table, a canvas bright,
With oranges, limes, a colorful sight.
A grapefruit squirted, made a bold splash,
While tangerines rolled, all in a dash!

A lemon dipped its toes in paint,
Said, "Look at my design, it's quaint!"
With strokes of zest, they made quite a mess,
A masterpiece formed, oh so express!

Each fruit took turns with a brush in hand,
Creating a world that was simply grand.
The colors blended, a flavorful spree,
Making art in a way only fruits can see!

And as they finished, they danced around,
In their pretty gallery, joy was found.
With every splash and every cheer,
The canvas burst with laughter, so clear!

Citrus Synthesis

In the orchard, lemons play,
Sipping sunshine, bright and gay.
Oranges juggling high in trees,
Grapefruits giggle in the breeze.

Limes wear hats of leafy green,
Telling jokes, they're quite the scene.
Pineapples dance with piney flair,
Sharing laughter everywhere.

Citrus fruits in fine ballet,
Turning sour into a sway.
With every splash of zesty zest,
Turning boredom into fest!

When they mingle on a plate,
Guava shrieks, "I'm feeling great!"
Pulp and juice, they start to rhyme,
In this wacky, fruity time.

Sun-Kissed Echoes

Sunkissed skins and playful pranks,
Tangerines in vibrant ranks.
Lemonade waves that splash and giggle,
Bouncing off tree trunks like a wiggle.

Oranges roll, a merry chase,
Lemons wear the silliest grace.
In the sun, they plot and scheme,
Creating quite a citrus dream.

When summer's heat begins to play,
They form a band and sing hooray!
With every slice and spurt of juice,
They dance together, let loose!

Join the fun, don't miss the show,
In this bright, zesty expo.
For in this orchard, all is fine,
With every laugh, we sip a lime.

The Flavorful Muse

A muse of fruit, so bold and bright,
Inspires chefs both day and night.
With zesty lines and punchy rhymes,
She whips up magic every time.

Lemon twists in every dish,
A tasty side that's hard to miss.
Cleanup's fun, they splash like sprites,
Creating chaos in the bites.

From tart to sweet, the flavors blend,
Zingy notes that never end.
In her kitchen, smiles abound,
Juicy ideas spin around!

Tarts and pies, a delectable trend,
With silly faces, all pretend.
In this fruity tale we weave,
Join the feast, just take a leave!

Juicy Stories of Summer

In a bowl of fruit, tales collide,
Melons roll on a juicy ride.
Citrus quirks with every bite,
Stories burst with every light.

Lemon jesters in the sun,
Slice them thick, oh what fun!
Oranges tell of sunny days,
In zesty laughs, they sing their praise.

Pineapples wear their crowns with glee,
Tropical tales shared by the sea.
With every sip of summer's cheer,
We gather 'round, the fun is near!

So grab a slice, come take a seat,
In this fruity realm, a juicy treat.
With laughter shared and smiles bright,
These stories glow in summer light.

The Squeeze of Life

In the garden, fruits collide,
Lemons giggle, oranges slide.
A grapefruit frowns, he's feeling neglected,
While tangerines dance, oh so connected.

Juice drips down, a playful mess,
Pulp fights back, Oh, what a stress!
Limes are laughing, mocking the plight,
"Just squeeze it out, and you'll be alright!"

Citrus jokes that never fail,
A zesty punchline, a fruity tale.
Peels fly high, like confetti in air,
Life's a party, if you dare!

With fruit hats on, they start to cheer,
"Don't be sour, bring on the beer!"
A lemon slice in a glass held tight,
Cheers to laughter, from morning till night!

A Peel Away from Ordinary

An orange rolls upon the floor,
A silly grin, who could ignore?
Lemons are plotting, a prank in the mix,
While limes just giggle, creating new tricks.

A zesty twist is how we thrive,
Banana peels make us come alive!
In a world that's often dull and gray,
Fruits unite, come join the fray!

We'll pelt each other with citrus zest,
Creating laughter, we must confess.
With every peel, a new surprise,
Lemon laughter fills the skies.

Let's ditch the boring, take a chance,
With fruity friends, we twirl and dance.
So grab a slice, make life a blast,
In this fruity world, we'll have a blast!

Zesty Encounters

Met a lime in a crowded bar,
Said, "I'm here, I'm quite bizarre!"
He told me stories of lemon fights,
Of fruity nights and zesty flights.

A grapefruit chimed in, quite the sage,
"Don't worry, it's all the same stage."
"All's fair in love and in fruit, my friend,
It's laughter and juice, they always blend."

With every sip, gaiety awaits,
Orange and lime have peculiar traits.
In this realm, there's no denying,
Where every taste leads to funny dying!

A twist of fate, a splash of juice,
Embrace the taste, there's no excuse.
For every bite, a laugh in store,
Zesty encounters, can't ask for more!

The Bright Side of Sours

In a world of sweet and tart,
Sour faces play a crucial part.
"Cheer up!" says the grapefruit, quite bold,
"Life's too short to be controlled!"

Lemons ponder, "What's the fuss?"
When bitterness leads, what's the plus?
But then they chuckle, realizing fate,
Their tangy charm makes life first-rate.

A pomelo sighed, brushed off the gray,
With zestful laughter, they came out to play.
Sour pusses turn their frowns upside down,
Even the pith can sport a crown!

So join the laugh, don't be a bore,
Find the sweetness in every sore.
For every sour has a story to tell,
The bright side of sours rings a joyous bell!

The Acid Was Sweet

In the land of zesty dreams,
Orange peels danced like beams.
Lemons chuckled in the sun,
Sour faces, oh what fun!

Grapefruit giggled on the vine,
Sipping laughter, feeling fine.
Limes rolled over, bright and bold,
Tales of tangy joys retold.

Mangoes watched with wide-eyed glee,
Whispering jokes from a citrus tree.
Every twist, a pucker made,
In a fruity masquerade!

So raise a glass, let laughter burst,
In this orchard, fun's the first.
With every slice, a smile's treat,
In this world where acid's sweet.

Citrus Reverie

In a grove where fruits collide,
Tangerines rolled, full of pride.
Lemons wore a sunny grin,
As limes shot jokes like a spin.

Grapefruit thinks it's quite the star,
Pondering if it's too bizarre.
Squeeze the humor, add some zest,
In this game, we're all the best.

Orange peels slip on the ground,
Laughter echoes all around.
Bananas smile, they don't mind,
In this joyful, tangy grind.

So come and taste this zesty lore,
Where giggles bloom and spirits soar.
In citrus dreams, the fun is real,
With every wedge, we share the feel.

Mellowed by Lemons

In a lemonade stand, quite the sight,
Lemons chatting through the night.
Jokes on the curb, they twist and turn,
For every laugh, a lemon's return.

One sly lime, with a wink and nod,
Told a tale that left us awed.
"Why did the orange stop in place?
It found its zest now, what a grace!"

Grapefruit grinned, adding spice,
"Please don't ask me, I'm not that nice!"
Under the stars, they laughed out loud,
In a mellow mood, they felt so proud.

So let us sip this tangy brew,
Where every lemon shares a cue.
Life's too sour, let's sweeten the day,
With jokes from fruits that always play.

Orchard Under Moonlight

In the orchard, moonbeams dance,
Peeling laughter, taking a chance.
Lemons giggle, oranges glow,
Secrets shared where night winds blow.

Grapefruit, a jester, wears a crown,
Spinning tales, wearing a frown.
But just beneath that fruity mask,
Laughter lurks, a playful task.

Limes toss whispers, so absurd,
Making jokes that sound unheard.
Amidst the fruits, joy takes flight,
Under the stars, oh what a sight!

So let us frolic under sky,
Where every fruit gets to apply.
Orchard vibes, a laughter spree,
In moonlit nights, we feel so free.

A Tapestry of Flavor

Lemons in the sun, laughing bright,
Juicy smiles and zesty bites.
Limes doing the tango, oh what a sight,
Fruits in a party, pure delight!

Oranges dress up in polka dots,
You think they're shy? Oh, they're not!
With peels as capes, they spin and twirl,
Making the whole fruit bowl whirl!

Grapefruits sing with a sassy tone,
Witty remarks, they've made it their own.
Each slice a punchline, oh so sweet,
In this fruity circus, life's a treat!

Together they dance, a bold parade,
In their zesty kingdom, laughter's made.
Turn up the fun, let flavors collide,
On this fruity journey, come take a ride!

When Life Hands You Oranges

When life gives you oranges, don't just pout,
Make a juggling act, let fun break out!
Chase your friend, toss one in the air,
Watch it roll away, oh, do beware!

Get some juice and splash it around,
Paint each other orange, oh what a sound!
Squeeze those laughs, let the freshness in,
With every giggle, let the fun begin!

Orange peels as hats, it's a sight to see,
Dancing together, wild and free.
Life's a comedy, just play your part,
With zesty passion, you'll win every heart!

So grab your oranges, let's make some cheer,
With fruity antics that bring us near.
After all, in this funny dance,
Every citrus slice deserves a chance!

Sweet and Sour Serenade

A sweet serenade from a limey lad,
Folk dancing while the oranges are mad.
With a squeeze and a twist, the mood turns bright,
In this wacky world, there's no room for fright!

Grapefruits croon, their tone so sly,
Cracking up lemons as they pass by.
With a tart little joke and a zesty pun,
This fruit medley always has fun!

Tangerines play hide and seek with zest,
While limes give high fives, feeling so blessed.
Under the sun, they sing their song,
In this merry mash, where all belong!

So let's raise a cup, a toast to the crew,
For every giggle and flavor so true.
In this funny garden, we all unite,
With sweet and sour laughter lighting the night!

Splashes of Citrus

Splashes of citrus bring joy to the day,
With every squirt, worries drift away.
In a citrus splash fight, we let it flow,
Oh, the sticky giggles, they steal the show!

Lemons line up for a cannonball dive,
Orange is laughing, feeling alive.
With a splash and a squirt, a fruity parade,
This juicy mayhem is surely well-made!

Toss a lime in, watch the fun go wild,
Zesty laughter, every adult and child.
Fruit-colored smiles, spreading so wide,
In this splashing game, we take pride!

So join the fun, don't hesitate,
Dance in the puddles before it's too late.
With zestful spirits and joy on display,
We'll celebrate life in a fruity way!

A Dance of Mandarins

In the orchard where the mandarins play,
They twirl and they twist in a zesty ballet.
With peels as bright as a cheerful sun,
They giggle and dance, just having fun.

One orange tripped on a lemon's peel,
It spun like a top, oh what a reel!
A lime jumped in, declaring, 'I'm cool!'
But slipped on his juice and fell in a pool.

The tangy tunes filled the air with delight,
As they jiggled and jived through the warm, starry night.
With laughter and juice all around,
The fruity fiesta was joyfully crowned.

So if you stroll through that orchard so bright,
Join the mandarin dance, it's pure delight!
Just watch for the slips, and if you fall,
Remember, my friend, it's the best dance of all!

The Lush Lemon Grove

In a grove where lemons grow thick and round,
Sour faces burst with laughter, abound.
Each fruit tells a tale of the sun's embrace,
With zesty jokes that quicken the pace.

A lemon tried to tell a joke so fine,
But slipped on a peel, said, 'I'm on cloud nine!'
With a squirt of juice and a zany grin,
It became the punchline—the fun could begin!

The trees all chuckled, leaves shaking in glee,
While bees buzzed around, joining the spree.
A sweet little lime said, 'Let's sing out loud!'
While the lemons formed a giggling crowd.

In this luscious grove, where humor is ripe,
Each fruit has its flair, like their own hype.
So pick a fresh lemon, and you will see,
Sour or sweet, there's joy, that's the key!

Ripened Thoughts

Under the sun, where ideas take flight,
Fruits ponder their meanings, day and night.
A grapefruit mused, 'Am I sweet or sour?'
While a tangerine checked her zest at the hour.

A pomelo proclaimed, 'I'm the belle of the ball!'
With a wink to the lime, who felt rather small.
'I know who I am!' said a bold little pear,
But fell from the branch—oh, what a scare!

A fruit salad party was planned in a rush,
But the strawberries blushed at a big, juicy crush.
Banter around bowls gets a little absurd,
While bananas slip in, with their gossip unheard.

So ripened thoughts float on the breeze,
As fruits share their tales, hoping you'll please.
Join the chatter, let laughter impart,
In the orchard of whimsy, we'll fill every heart!

Taste of Sunshine

When life gives you fruit, take a big, sweet bite,
Laughter dances in flavors, oh what a delight!
Mangoes wearing sunglasses, chill on the scenes,
While strawberries giggle, bursting at the seams.

The taste of sunshine in every zing,
With pivots and swirls, let the laughter ring.
A bite of a tangerine brings forth a chime,
And suddenly fruit salad turns into crime!

Fruits marching boldly, in parades of delight,
Lemurs join the fun, being quirky and bright.
With apples that joust, and pears that might dance,
This jolly buffet is the best kind of chance!

So dig into sunshine, and savor the cheer,
With each zesty giggle, your worries disappear.
Life's sweet and sour, a scrumptious affair,
So gather your fruits, let's take to the air!

Sweetness Beneath the Skin

Peeling back the layers, oh so bright,
A zesty surprise that takes flight.
Pudding on the floor, I dance with glee,
A lemon slice just slipped on me!

Juicy giggles, oh what a treat,
Sour tangs make my day complete.
With every squirt that brings delight,
I wear a grin, oh what a sight!

The fruit bowl's jester, I reign supreme,
Chasing after my citrus dream.
A mishap here, a squish there,
In this game of zest, I have flair!

But when the seeds invade my bliss,
Each tiny prick feels like a hiss.
Yet still I laugh, I can't resist,
For sweetness beneath, does persist!

Citrus Hues of Happiness

Sunshine drops in shades of gold,
Grapefruits giggle, tales unfold.
Tangerine twirls, a merry sight,
Bursting colors in the light!

Lemons wear the crown so high,
Dancing on clouds, oh me, oh my!
Lime joins in with sparkling cheer,
Mixing joy, year after year.

In the market, I skip and hop,
Each corner I turn, sweet pops and plops.
The zesty smell, oh it's divine,
I might just squeeze myself some lime!

Bananas slip away in fright,
While citrus laughs till the night.
With vibrant hues, they paint the sky,
In this fruity world, who needs to fly?

The Limoncello Lament

Oh, sweet elixir, where did you go?
Left my heart with a bitter woe.
I searched the fridge, I looked inside,
But all I found was pickle pride!

A shot of joy, now lost in time,
Missing your sparkle, your essence sublime.
I made a toast to empty air,
To dreams of sipping without a care!

Each citrus squeeze brings back the fun,
But now my glass is on the run.
A bottle cap with no surprise,
It vanished quick before my eyes!

Yet here I dance amidst the jest,
As lemons groan, they know me best.
I'll find my drink, come what may,
In this limoncello cabaret!

Forgotten Zing

Once a zestful spark, now a fade,
In the bottom drawer, the colors degrade.
Oranges mellowed under the bed,
Forgotten dreams swirl in my head.

With every sniff, a memory wakes,
Sour days filled with silly mistakes.
When zestful fights caught us in laughter,
And citrus games echoed thereafter!

I pull them out, a citrus parade,
With giggles and screams, they won't evade.
The fuzzy, old lemons hold a grudge,
Yet I find joy, I cannot budge!

So here we are, the once astringent crew,
Creating sunshine, making do.
Even when life gives a bitter sting,
We'll dance and laugh, we found our zing!

A Canvas of Peels

In a world where fruit's a fool,
Lemons dance, they break the rule.
Oranges juggle with their zest,
While grapefruits claim they are the best.

A splash of juice, a squirt of fun,
Mangoes laugh, they've just begun.
Limes are cheeky, oh so bright,
Throwing parties every night.

Bananas slip, in classic style,
Citrus chuckles, all the while.
Peels on the floor, a vibrant sight,
Watch your step, it's quite the plight.

So with a grin and sunny cheer,
Dance with fruit, have no fear.
The canvas bright, a juicy feel,
Life's a joke, it's all surreal.

Fragrant Horizons

A scent of orange fills the air,
Limes and lemons everywhere.
Tangerines leap with delight,
Inviting friends to join the night.

The grapefruits wear a dandy hat,
While citron jokes, "I'm quite the cat!"
Each slice reveals a burst of glee,
Fragrant horizons, wild and free.

Peel back laughter, layer it thick,
Life's a fruit salad, take your pick.
With every zesty, tangy note,
Join the fun, let's rock the boat!

In this land of juicy puns,
Crack a smile, join in the runs.
Our fruity friends, a merry crew,
Fragrant horizons, all anew.

Pith and Promise

Beneath the peel, a secret lies,
Pithy jokes that provoke sighs.
Each juicy drop a tale to tell,
Of sunny days and citrus swell.

Promises squeezed in every bite,
Pith and zest, they share the light.
Bitter rinds and sweet in cheer,
Fragrant laughter, let's adhere.

A lemonade stand in a tilt,
Grapes giggle, "It's not our guilt!"
Meanwhile, juicers grind with glee,
Pulp in hand, just let it be.

So raise your glass to fun and cheer,
Fridge full of fruit, bring it near.
Pith and promise, what a mix,
Squeeze out joy, it's life's cool fix.

The Color of Flavor

Yellow sunbeams in a glass,
Citrus colors come to pass.
Orange smiles and lemon flair,
Every sip, a flavor dare.

Fruits on parade, a splashy scene,
Tart and sweet, they reign supreme.
Drawn to laughter, zestful glee,
Colors bright as they can be.

Pinks and greens that spin and twirl,
Citrus wonders, watch them whirl.
So grab a slice, don't hesitate,
Join the show, it's never late.

From lemonade to marmalade,
Every taste, a new charade.
The color of flavor, bright and true,
Laughter blended just for you.

The Color of Flavor

In a world of zest and glee,
Lemonade spills from the tree.
Limes giggle in their green delight,
While oranges dance to the fruit stand's light.

Tangerines don a peel so bright,
Pretending to be stars in the night.
Grapefruits sing with a cheeky grin,
Squeezing laughter from their thick skin.

Pineapples wear crowns and prance,
Inviting others to join their dance.
Together they laugh, a fruity array,
In a carnival of flavor play!

So grab a slice, let's get bold,
Sweet stories of fruit will unfold.
In this land of vibrant cheer,
Every bite brings a smile near!

Sunkissed Journeys

Underneath the sun's bright call,
Lemons roll and tumble, having a ball.
Each twist creates a giggle so sweet,
As they chase each other down the street.

A grapefruit made a daring leap,
Over a melon, making us weep.
"Oh, let's squeeze the day!" they cry,
With zestful shouts as they pass by.

Onward they roll, their mission clear,
To find some friends for a sunny cheer.
They met a lime with a ticklish jest,
And surely knew they'd all be blessed.

Together they juggle under the sun,
A fruity circus that's just for fun.
With laughter ringing in the air,
Sunkissed journeys beyond compare!

Tangelo Trysts

In orchards bright with glee galore,
Tangelos plot behind a door.
"Let's meet at dawn for our grand jest,
To bring the lemons to the test!"

Sneaky peels and crafty schemes,
They'll paint their world in juicy dreams.
Hiding from prying eyes so keen,
Giggling softly, a fruity scene.

With every twist and every turn,
In the game of zest, they take their turn.
Sour and sweet in a playful dance,
They whirl about in a citrus romance.

The day concludes with laughter so hearty,
With tangy treats to end the party.
In this fruit-filled land of bliss,
It's tangelo hugs they surely miss!

Orange Blossom Serenade

In an orchard lush, with blossoms bold,
An orange band sings stories untold.
With each note, they sway and spin,
Creating tunes that make you grin.

Lively petals flutter in the breeze,
Citrus laughter floats with ease.
Lemons tap their little feet,
As all the fruits unite to greet.

"Join us!" they sing, in harmony bright,
For a serenade under the moonlight.
Their zestful chorus fills the air,
Bringing joy and laughter everywhere.

As twilight falls, they do not cease,
The vibrant fruits share their peace.
In the warm embrace, they all agree,
That life's a song, so sweet and free!

Zesty Secrets

In sunny realms where fruits do play,
Limes and lemons dance all day.
They whisper jokes upon the breeze,
Sour confessions with such ease.

Oranges chuckle, vibrant and round,
Sharing laughter, oh what a sound!
A grapefruit grins, it's quite the show,
With each juicy bite, the humor flows.

Lemonade stands but a clever guise,
For fruit's wit hides behind bright skies.
Each zest has tales, funny and bright,
In the orchard, all's pure delight.

So peel a slice, come join the fun,
Squeeze a giggle, let's all run!
In every segment, a smile's disguise,
Nature's punchlines in colorful ties.

From Tree to Table

Pick an orange, ripe and bold,
Juicy tales the fruit has told.
From branches high to kitchen bright,
The journey's filled with sheer delight.

With every twist, with every peel,
A zesty joke that's truly real.
Pineapple crowns wear the hat,
While lemons laugh, 'Where's the plat?'

Swinging by, the fruits parade,
Bananas slip, oh what a trade!
Grapefruit rolls with a cheeky grin,
Saying, "Add a slice, let's begin!"

As fruit bowls fill, the laughter thrives,
Squeezed into juice, our joy arrives.
From tree to table, what a trip,
Life's zesty moments in every sip.

Drifting on Citrus Clouds

Floating high on sunny dreams,
Lemon meringue in shining beams.
Tangerines, like cotton candy,
Give soft giggles all so dandy.

With each sweet puff, a citrus cheer,
Bouncing laughter through the year.
Mandarins swing, a playful bunch,
Gliding by with a citrus crunch.

Juicy jokes in whimsical weather,
Limes and oranges, laugh together.
On fluffy clouds, they twist and twirl,
Creating zest in a fruity whirl.

So grab a slice, let's float around,
In this world of laughter found.
From skies above, the fruit confides,
Drifting bliss on zesty tides.

The Bounty of Bloom

In orchards lush, a colorful sight,
Fruits made jests in the warm daylight.
A berry blushed, a cherry grinned,
While apples laughed, their tales to spin.

Pineapples joke about their crown,
While juicy pears never frown.
Each bloom a secret, bright and fun,
With every petal, joy begun.

Citrusy laughter fills the air,
As veggies sigh, 'It's just not fair!'
In gardens blooming with fruity charm,
Nature weaves her humorous yarn.

So gather 'round the harvest tide,
Where every bite brings joy and pride.
The bounty's rich, the laughter spry,
In the fruit-filled world, we soar so high.

Zestful Whispers

In the kitchen, a lemon grins,
Rolling round, it always wins.
It bounces here, it bounces there,
Squeezing laughter with its flair.

Oh, the peels that land on floors,
Peeled bananas start some wars.
The fruit bowl holds a funny crew,
All in a race, who knew?!

Lime jokes are just too tart,
They try but never win the part.
Grapefruits frown with such disdain,
But the oranges, they entertain.

So here's to fruit that makes us smile,
With every joke, we'll savor the style.
A citrus twist, we share a laugh,
Juicy tales, we'll always half!

The Tang of Time

Time flies, just like a lime,
Wobbling low on the kitchen rhyme.
It laughs at you, it rolls away,
Showing up later, 'Oh hey!'

Next come oranges in a hat,
Sipping juice, oh what's up with that?
Citrus dance-offs in the sun,
Makin' jokes, it's all in fun.

A tangerine tries to crack a pun,
But ends up rolling, what a run!
Peels scattered with pure delight,
Who knew fruit could be so bright?

Lemons joke about their zest,
In a fruit bowl, they're the best!
A slice of funny on your plate,
Let's peel back laughs, it's never late!

Sun-Kissed Oranges

Sun-kissed oranges hold a cheer,
With silly grins, they draw us near.
Wobbling to a funky beat,
They shimmy down with juicy feet.

Mandarins giggle, oh can't you see?
They play hide and seek with glee.
Which one's peeled, which one's whole?
They laugh together, that's their role.

A jolly fruit flew up the wall,
Took a tumble, what a sprawl!
In a smoothie, they take a dive,
Fruity fun keeps us alive!

With every squeeze comes funny juice,
Making moments, we can't refuse.
Sun-kissed laughter, oh what bliss,
A citrus hug you wouldn't miss!

Slices of Sunshine

Slices dancing on the plate,
Sunshine fruit can't be late.
Each one winks, each one plays,
Shouting cheers for sunny days.

Pineapple jokes, they're quite the charm,
With a silly grin, they disarm.
Mangoes roll into the street,
Chasing laughter with fruity feet.

Watermelon cracks a smile,
Juicy bites go on for a while.
Peachy puns flying in the air,
What a fruity, vibrant fair!

A bunch of slices in a row,
Time for laughter, off we go!
Sunny moments, let them shine,
In our hearts, all things divine!

Orchard Conversations

In the grove, the oranges joke,
Lemons laugh, and grapefruits choke.
"You're so sour, you should be warred!"
"At least I'm not just a fridge's hoard!"

The limes roll eyes with zest so bright,
Saying, "C'mon, it's just a bite!"
But lemons know they can't complain,
They're just too used to all the disdain!

Tangerines in a peppy dance,
"Hey, look at us! We take a chance!"
Pineapples shake with a lofty clout,
"Just don't put me in a pizza, no doubt!"

Grapes all gossip while on the vine,
"Do you think we'll get a grapevine sign?"
A pear pipes up, "Oh please, I crave,
A chance to roll and be quite brave!"

Rays of Tangy Light

Morning sun spills like juice on skins,
Bananas grin; it's where fun begins.
"Let's peel back the dawn," they say,
"Chasing away the gloom of gray!"

Tangerines twirl in the golden hue,
While clementines chatter, "What's new with you?"
"Did you hear about the peach's talk?
She said we're the stars of the fruit brick walk!"

Underneath trees, mischief abound,
With every splash, new laughter is found.
A grapefruit slips into a core of mirth,
Causing giggles to bounce off the earth!

So come, gather under that bright sunlight,
Where citrus dreams soar in playful flight.
Weaving tales of zest and delight,
In a world where fruits taste just right!

Zestful Journeys

Let's pack our bags with juicy treats,
On this adventure, no one retreats.
"The road calls us!" shouts a fresh lime,
"We'll travel far; it'll be sublime!"

Past orchards bright and valleys wide,
With a fruit salad as our guide.
"Be careful of the slippery peel!"
Said one brave pear, with zest to feel.

Under rainbows, we'll dance and sing,
Bringing joy that the sunshine can bring.
"Where to next?" asks a curious berry,
"To the land where tangy dreams can tarry!"

So off we go, with laughter and cheer,
Spreading zest through every frontier.
In this conga of fruits, we unite,
On zestful journeys, forever in flight!

The Tang of Dawn

Every morning brings a jolly surprise,
A tangy burst to stir sleepy eyes.
"Wake up, sleepyheads, what a sight!"
cried mangoes, glowing in morning's light.

Pineapples dance atop the hill,
Ensuring morning's laughter, a stunning thrill.
"Grab your peeler, let's get this right,
For breakfast calls with zestful delight!"

Grapefruits chime in with a toast,
"Here's to those who love us most!"
With noisy cheer, the fruit brigade,
Transforms dawn with joy that won't fade!

So as day unfolds, grab your slice,
Join this cheerful, zest-filled life.
With each new dawn, we'll sing our song,
In the orchard's heart, where we belong!

Whirls of Citrus Dreams

In the land of zesty schemes,
Lemons giggle in the beams.
Oranges roll with sly grins,
A fruit fiesta, let the fun begin!

Juggling limes in silly hats,
Dancing pears with acrobats.
Grapefruits sing a merry tune,
Underneath a laughing moon.

Fruits wear shoes to run and play,
Sour faces turn to yay!
A tangerine slips on the floor,
And rolls right out the open door!

Citrus pals with bright delight,
Join together, oh what a sight!
With every splash of juice and cheer,
They fill the world with laughter here.

In the Shade of Fruit

Under trees where fruits do collide,
Lemons gossip, oranges bide.
Grapefruit spreads tales quite absurd,
As apples roll, lost for the word!

Limes tell jokes that leave us green,
While peaches blush, a sweet scene.
Melons chuckle, seeds fly high,
Their laughter echoes to the sky.

In a citrus brawl, who'll win?
A juicy battle, a playful sin.
With every squeeze, the giggles rise,
As tangy zest fills up the skies.

The sun dips low, colors abound,
In this fruity circus, laughter's found.
Merry moments, the shade is bright,
As fruits unite in sheer delight.

Radiant Peel

Peeling back the laughs inside,
Zesty layers, oh what a ride!
Bananas slip, and oranges swing,
In this fiesta, joy's the king!

Minty hints and tangy sparks,
Grapes take flight like little larks.
Peels that dance, and laughter burst,
In this citrus world, we quench our thirst.

Every slice brings silly glee,
A fruit parade for you and me.
With fragrant zest and fizzy cheers,
We celebrate the fun-filled years.

So let's zest up this grand affair,
With puns and giggles, everywhere.
Radiant peels, funny and bright,
In this fruity world, all feels right.

Golden Drops of Joy

Dripping sunshine from the sky,
Marmalade clouds, oh my oh my!
Lemon drops and tangerine trails,
As laughter flows, the happiness swells.

Orange juice rivers run with glee,
While limes tell tales of mystery.
In this land where sweetness reigns,
Funny antics course through our veins.

A grapefruit wears a silly crown,
While pineapples dance all around.
Sugar and zest collide in a swirl,
A radiant circle, a fruity whirl.

Golden drops, a joy parade,
In every squeeze, fun is made.
With each sweet bite, the laughter soars,
In this fruity haven, joy restores.

Tangy Reflections

In a kitchen, loud and bright,
Oranges dance in morning light.
Lemons giggle, full of zest,
Lime slices wearing polka-dot vests.

Juicy puns fly through the air,
Fruit jokes tumble, beware—beware!
Limey laughter, mixed and sweet,
Peeling oranges, a zany treat.

A splash of juice, a funny face,
Citrusy chaos at a lively pace.
Sipping laughter from a cup,
In this fruit fest, we never stop.

With every slice, a giggling cheer,
Citrus capers, lend an ear.
Tart delight in every bite,
In this fruit bowl, joy takes flight.

The Golden Teardrops

Lemon drops on cheeks do roam,
Sour faces call this place home.
In a bowl so round and bright,
Fruits conspire under the light.

A zesty dance, they whirl and sway,
Squeezed-out laughs in their own way.
Mocking shadows, citrus play,
Joyful spritzes mark the day.

Orange giggles dribble down,
From each twist, there's not a frown.
Sour meets sweet in this delight,
Each fruit claims its fruity right.

In a blender, laughter churns,
Sweet and tart, the fruit world turns.
Golden humor bursts in cheer,
In this fruity world, we persevere.

Echoes of Grapefruit

Grapefruits sing in shades of fun,
Harmonies spark under the sun.
With every bite, a burst of cheer,
Echoes of laughter for all to hear.

Sour notes meet a sugary tone,
In this duet, we're never alone.
Juicy verses on taste buds play,
In citrus melodies, we sway.

Fuzzy skins in cheerful rows,
Slicing through, the giggle grows.
A twist of jests in every round,
Citrus echoes, joy is found.

Count the seeds, or lose the plot,
In this fruit bowl, we care not.
Grapefruit giggles fill the air,
In fruit-filled songs, we all share.

Sweetness in the Air

Tangerines bounce with flair,
In the kitchen, sweetness in the air.
Mischief mingles, fresh and bright,
Across the counter, what a sight!

Pineapple crowns with leafy grace,
Fruity mischief takes its place.
Chopping limes, a wacky affair,
Sour giggles float everywhere.

Juicy whispers fill each nook,
Fruit baskets smiling like a book.
Every slice a story shares,
In this sweet world, laughter dares.

Peeling laughter, tangy surprise,
In citrus corners, fun complies.
Banana splits and silly puns,
In our fruit zone, the joy outruns.

Sweetness in the Shade

In the grove where lemons laugh,
Limes are plotting their sweet path.
Oranges roll and play all day,
While grapefruits try to steal the play.

Squirrels sneak a taste or two,
Hiding snacks, oh what a view!
With sun hats made from lemon leaves,
They toast to life with giggles and thieves.

Peeling Back the Sunrise

Peel an orange, watch it shine,
The juice drips like a silly line.
Morning's here with zesty cheer,
   Citrus jokes are all we hear.

A lemon joked, 'I'm quite a zest!',
A lime replied, 'You're not the best!'
Together they made quite a team,
Sour and sweet, living the dream.

Sunburst Reverie

In the sun where lemons glimmer,
Mandarins dance, their smiles shimmer.
Each fruity laugh, a jolly sound,
As they gather 'round the playground.

Watermelons try to join the fun,
But slide right off, oh what a run!
Juicy tales of epic bounces,
Zesty laughter, joy surmounts.

Zestful Echoes of August

In August hues, the fruits unite,
Mangoes swinging, what a sight!
Zestful tunes from folky vines,
Melodies mixed with sweet-tart lines.

Lemons throw a party bold,
With tangerines, tales unfold.
Sipping punch with gummy bears,
Citrus highs and funny airs.

www.ingramcontent.com/pod-product-compliance
Lightning Source LLC
Chambersburg PA
CBHW070316120526
44590CB00017B/2705